D1709512

Rivers and Lakes

Lake Superior

John F. Prevost

ABDO Publishing Company

visit us at
www.abdopub.com

Published by ABDO Publishing Company, 4940 Viking Drive, Edina, Minnesota 55435.
Copyright © 2002 by Abdo Consulting Group, Inc. International copyrights reserved in
all countries. No part of this book may be reproduced in any form without written
permission from the publisher.

Printed in the United States.

Photo credits: Corbis

Contributing editors: Bob Italia, Tamara L. Britton, Kate A. Furlong, Kristin Van Cleaf
Book design and graphics: Neil Klinepier

Library of Congress Cataloging-in-Publication Data

Prevost, John F.
    Lake Superior / by John F. Prevost.
        p. cm. -- (Rivers and lakes)
    Includes bibliographical references and index.
    Summary: Surveys the origin, geological borders, climate, water,
plant and animal life, and economic and ecological aspects of Lake
Superior.
    ISBN 1-57765-104-9
    1. Superior, Lake--Juvenile literature. 2. Superior, Lake,
Region--Juvenile literature. [1. Superior, Lake.] I. Title.
II. Series.
F552.P74 1999
977.4'9--DC21   98-11983
                                                            CIP
                                                            AC

Contents

Lake Superior

Lake Superior lies along the border between Canada and the United States. It is the world's largest freshwater lake. It covers an area of 31,000 square miles (80,290 sq km).

Lake Superior is one of the five Great Lakes. The other Great Lakes are Huron, Ontario, Michigan, and Erie. Lake Superior is the largest, deepest, and coldest of these lakes.

All the Great Lakes are connected by rivers, canals, and **straits**. The St. Lawrence Seaway connects the Great Lakes with the Atlantic Ocean. This means goods loaded on a ship at Lake Superior can travel all the way to the Atlantic Ocean.

People have affected Lake Superior in many ways. Trappers, loggers, fishermen, and miners have all used many natural resources from the lake and its shores. Today, people are working to preserve the lake and its beautiful lands for the future.

Forming the Lake

Millions of years ago, large chunks of ice called glaciers formed in North America. The glaciers were large and heavy. Some glaciers were nearly two miles (3 km) thick!

Over time, the glaciers slowly drifted across the continent. They carved deep **basins** in the land. Glaciers formed Lake Superior's basin about 12,000 years ago. As the glaciers melted, fresh water filled the basin.

After the glaciers melted, the land around Lake Superior's basin slowly rose. It no longer had the weight of the glaciers pushing it down. As the land rose, it made Lake Superior's basin even deeper.

Today, Lake Superior's deep water is clear, cold, and pure. The water that fills Lake Superior comes from rain and snow. Nearly 200 nearby **tributaries** also drain water into the lake.

Lake Superior reached its current water level about 2,000 years ago.

Superior's Shores

The glaciers that formed Lake Superior also shaped the land surrounding it. The glaciers left Lake Superior with steep cliffs, rocky shores, and sandy beaches. The lake's shores are also covered in forests. The two kinds of forests that grow near the lake are boreal and deciduous.

Boreal forests are filled with evergreen trees. They cover the northern shores of Lake Superior. The most common kinds of trees in these forests are balsam fir and white spruce.

The southern shores of Lake Superior are covered with deciduous forests. They have trees that lose their leaves every autumn. Before this happens, the leaves turn bright shades of red, orange, and yellow.

Many animals live in Lake Superior's forests. Large animals such as black bears, deer, and wolves make their homes there. Snowshoe hares and porcupines live in the forests, too.

*The deciduous trees along Lake Superior have
brilliantly-colored leaves in the fall.*

Wildlife in the Water

Lake Superior's waters are home to many animals. Birds live on the lake in the summer. The most common birds are gulls, terns, and ducks. During the spring and fall, songbirds stop at Lake Superior while **migrating**.

Fish also live in Lake Superior. Some of these fish include pike, perch, trout, bass, and muskellunge. These fish were abundant in Lake Superior for thousands of years.

Then humans built waterways to connect the Great Lakes and the Atlantic Ocean. Sea lamprey swam from the Atlantic to the Great Lakes. They arrived in Lake Superior in 1948. Soon, the sea lamprey had killed nearly all of the lake's trout.

The lamprey upset the balance of Lake Superior's **ecosystem**. To fix this problem, scientists put chemicals into the lake's **tributaries**. The lamprey bred in these waterways. The chemicals killed most of the lamprey. Scientists then restocked the lake with trout.

A mallard duck and her ducklings wade into Lake Superior.

Lakeside Weather

*L*ake Superior has a major effect on local weather. In the spring and summer, Lake Superior's waters **absorb** heat. This makes the land near the lake cooler.

In the fall months, especially November, there are great wind storms over the lake. These winds are called gales. They can cause waves more than 10 feet (3 m) high!

Gales on Lake Superior have caused many shipwrecks. One of the lake's most famous shipwrecks was that of the *Edmund Fitzgerald*. This iron-**ore** carrier and its entire crew sank during a wind storm on November 10, 1975.

In the winter, Lake Superior causes heavy snowfall. This happens when cold, winter air passes over the warm lake. Moisture from the warm lake **evaporates** into the cold air. The moisture cools, forms clouds, and falls to the ground as snow. This is called lake-effect snow.

Lake-effect snow usually falls within 20 to 30 miles (32 to 48 km) of shore. This area is called a snowbelt.

First Settlers

Native Americans were the first people to settle on the land near Lake Superior. The Ojibwa, also called the Chippewa, lived along the rapids at St. Marys River. This river flows out of Lake Superior. Later, the Ojibwa moved closer to the lake.

The Ojibwa had much respect for Lake Superior. They called it *Kitchi Gami,* which means Great Ocean. The Ojibwa traveled on *Kitchi Gami* and its **tributaries** in birch bark canoes.

The Ojibwa lived in wigwams. These dome-shaped homes were made of saplings covered with birch bark. Ojibwa women carried the wigwams with them as the tribe moved around the lake in search of food.

The Ojibwa were not the only Native Americans who lived near Lake Superior. Other tribes that lived near the lake included the Cree, Dakota, Menominee, and Potawatomie.

Today, many Ojibwa traditions are still carried on by tribal members such as this man, who makes a birch bark canoe.

Explorers

*F*rench explorer Étienne Brûlé was the first European to see Lake Superior. He arrived at the lake in about 1622. Other French and English explorers soon came to the area.

The Europeans traded with the Native Americans. The Europeans offered tools, guns, and cloth in exchange for beaver furs. They shipped the furs to Europe, where they were used to make hats and coats. The fur trade quickly became an important industry in the Lake Superior area.

During the early 1800s, the fur trade near Lake Superior slowed. The beavers had been overhunted and few remained. So the European settlers began looking to Lake Superior's other resources to earn a living.

Fishermen created a large industry from Lake Superior's plentiful supply of fish. Miners began removing iron **ore**, copper, and gold from the land near the lake's shores. Loggers cut down trees in the forests to use for lumber and paper.

European explorers valued the beaver's warm fur.

Lake Superior Today

*T*oday, about one million people live near Lake Superior. Most of these people live on the U.S. side of the lake. The major cities on the lake are Thunder Bay, Ontario, and Duluth, Minnesota.

Duluth and Superior, Wisconsin, share a harbor. Its ports are some of the busiest in the U.S. Every day, ships from around the world come to these ports. They transport tons of raw materials, such as iron **ore** and grains.

Tourism is another important part of Lake Superior today. In the summer, visitors come to fish, boat, hike, and camp. In the winter, people come to cross-country ski and snowmobile.

Lake Superior is also a source of energy. The St. Marys River, which flows between Lake Superior and Lake Huron, has **locks** and dams along it. The dams provide electricity for the locks, as well as neighboring homes and businesses.

The **locks** along the St. Marys River are also important. They allow large ships to pass between Lake Superior and Lake Huron. Without these locks, large ships would not be able to travel to the other Great Lakes or the Atlantic Ocean.

An iron-ore boat at the Soo Lock along the St. Marys River

A Healthy Lake

*P*eople once thought that Lake Superior had an unlimited supply of natural resources such as furs, timber, minerals, and fish. Industries freely used these resources to make money.

Years of industry hurt Lake Superior and its land. Trappers reduced the beaver population during the fur trade. Loggers cut down large areas of forest. Miners removed many of the land's most valuable minerals. Fishermen caught so many fish that some species became extinct. Factories polluted the water and air.

Today, many industries are improving their ways. They have become more respectful of Lake Superior and its land. The Canadian and American governments are also working together to preserve the lake. These efforts have helped make Lake Superior the least polluted of all the Great Lakes. State and national parks on the lake's shores and islands also protect this massive lake for the future.

*On a calm day, it is possible to see more than 30 feet (9 m)
below the surface of Lake Superior's pure waters.*

Glossary

absorb - to take in or soak up.

basin - low-lying land.

ecosystem - a community of organisms and their environment.

evaporate - to change from a liquid into a vapor.

lock - a closed space on a river with gates on each end. It is used to raise or lower boats to different water levels along the river.

migrate - to travel in search of food or better weather conditions.

ore - a rock in the earth containing enough of a metal or mineral to make mining it profitable.

strait - a narrow waterway connecting two large bodies of water.

tributary - a river or stream that flows into a larger river, stream, or a lake.

How Do You Say That?

deciduous - dih-SIH-jeh-wehs
Étienne Brûlé - eht-YENN broo-LAY
Menominee - muh-NOM-uh-nee
muskellunge - MUHS-kuh-lunj
Ojibwa - oh-JIB-way
Potawatomie - pot-uh-WOT-uh-mee

Web Sites

Great Lakes Online
http://www.seagrant.wisc.edu/greatlakesonline/
Visitors to this site can learn about the birds, fish, and frogs of the Great Lakes. They can also explore underwater shipwrecks and discover fun science facts about the lakes.

Soo Locks Homepage
http://huron.lre.usace.army.mil/SOO/soohmpg.html
This site explains the history of the Soo Locks and how they work.

These sites are subject to change. Go to your favorite search engine and type in Lake Superior for more sites.

Index